T0145150

AS YOU GROW

DR. CHRISTINA KEMP

AuthorHouse™
1663 Liberty Drive
Bloomington, IN 47403
www.authorhouse.com
Phone: 833-262-8899

Because of the dynamic nature of the Internet, any web addresses or links contained in this book may have changed since publication and may no longer be valid. The views expressed in this work are solely those of the author and do not necessarily reflect the views of the publisher, and the publisher hereby disclaims any responsibility for them.

Any people depicted in stock imagery provided by Getty Images are models, and such images are being used for illustrative purposes only.
Certain stock imagery © Getty Images.

Illustrator: Nyomi Rose Edwards

This book is printed on acid-free paper.

ISBN: 978-1-6655-3905-0 (sc)
ISBN: 978-1-6655-3907-4 (hc)
ISBN: 978-1-6655-3906-7 (e)

Library of Congress Control Number: 2021919449

Print information available on the last page.

Published by AuthorHouse 10/20/2021

authorHOUSE

AS YOU GROW

What I want you to know as you grow is that you are as **STRONG** and **MIGHTY** as a T. rex.

Use your roar to speak up. You should always lift your head high and do the right thing.

SUPER DINO ROOARR!

What I want you to know as you grow is that you are as POWERFUL as the blue whale.

Swim far and wide. Your thoughts and ideas let you explore the world and can open any door.

What I want you to know as you grow is that you are as CLEVER as Batman. His superpower is his big, smart brain.

So put on your cape, try your best, and fly. Follow your dreams and goals wherever they take you.

What I want you to know as you grow is that you are as RESILIENT as the water bear. You can keep going when things around you are tough.

When you make a mistake or fail, get back up and try again.

What I want you to know as you grow is that **YOU ARE LOVED.** You are as precious as the rarest diamond.

Life can be unfair. People can be unkind and not always see you for who you really are.

What I want you to know as you grow is that there will always be someone smarter, faster, and bigger than you, but there is only one **YOU.**

Don't try to be anyone else. Be the best YOU that you can be, because YOU are pretty fantastic.

The world needs YOUR gifts and talents. Use them and share them with others.

Printed in the United States
by Baker & Taylor Publisher Services